Best-Ever Circle Time Activities: Back to School

50 Instant & Irresistible Meet-and-Greet Activities, Learning Games, and Language-Building Songs and Rhymes

By Ellen Booth Church

SCHOLASTIC
PROFESSIONAL BOOKS

NEW YORK • TORONTO • LONDON • AUCKLAND • SYDNEY
MEXICO CITY • NEW DELHI • HONG KONG • BUENOS AIRES

To Deborah Collette Murphy of the Dome School in Cave Junction, Oregon,
for all the joy of learning she continues to bring
to each new batch of children who walk through her door.

ACKNOWLEDGMENTS

I would like to thank Jerry Levine for his excellent assistance
with "tweaking" the rhymes in this book, and Linda Perline for the classroom ideas
she so lovingly shares with others.

Cover design by Gerard Fuchs
Interior design by Solutions by Design, Inc.
Interior illustrations by James Graham Hale

ISBN: 0-439-43114-X

4 5 6 7 8 9 10   40   08 07 06 05 04

Contents

Introduction

"Education is not a preparation for life;
education is life itself."
—John Dewey

Circle time is the heart of your program. And since it's the place where children meet, share, listen, and care, it's important to start off your year with well-planned circle-time activities that not only help kids get to know one another, but give them valuable experience in group learning. The skills you introduce in circle time now will sustain children all year and through their later schooling!

Imagine your beginning-of-the-year circles as a gathering place. You are gathering children—but you're also gathering much, much more. You are creating a confluence of individuals who bring with them diverse interests, abilities, cultures, and families. Each child arrives at your door with a rich heritage that can only enhance your program. The trick is to celebrate individuals—while at the same time creating community! Recent studies suggest that children who feel a sense of identity within their group are more successful in school. Your back-to-school circle time is the place where it all starts!

The activities in this book will strengthen children's sense of self while introducing them to others and to the joys of working, playing, and creating together. Think of this book as a quick and easy guide for ideas that will start the year off right. (Remember, you can always revisit the activities anytime throughout the year!)

Studies tell us that some of the most important skills children need for school success are "people" skills—social interaction, communication, collaboration, and problem solving. They are the fertile soil from which grows the "academics" of the ABC's and the 123's.

The activities in this book will help you as you tend your "circle-time garden" and sow the seeds that enable children to grow into avid learners.

This book is divided into four sections:

Welcoming Children
Circle-time activities for the first few days of school.

Getting to Know You
Help children get acquainted with one another with these activities.

The Three R's of Circle Time: Ritual, Routines, and Rules
Children feel more comfortable when they know what to expect! Help them get to know the daily schedule—and your expectations.

Creating a Circle-Time Community
Once kids get to know one another and are familiar with classroom routines, they can work beautifully together as a group. Help create a classroom community that will learn and grow together.

CIRCLE-TIME SKILLS

Every time you bring children together in your circle you are introducing, developing, and enriching skills in the educational domains of social, cognitive, language, and physical development. Just look at these skills your children use at circle time:

Pro-Social Development
- Self-esteem
- Name recognition
- Following directions
- Understanding routines
- Taking turns
- Cooperation
- Collaboration
- Manners
- Social interaction
- Sharing
- Organization
- Responsibility

Language Development
- Expressive language
- Vocabulary
- Listening
- Speaking
- Dictating
- Singing
- Phonemic awareness
- Sequencing
- Left-to-right progression
- Pre-reading and -writing

Physical Development
- Balance
- Gross motor coordination
- Fine motor coordination
- Creative movement

Cognitive Development
- Attending
- Memory
- Visual discrimination
- Matching
- Counting
- Inference
- Deduction
- Observation
- Sorting
- Creative thinking
- Comparing
- Predicting
- Problem solving

Terrific Tips for Getting Circle Time Started

◉ **Start with short** circle times. Leave them wanting more!

◉ **Don't require attendance**, but be so interesting that children just *have* to come over to see what is going on!

◉ **Keep a balance** of active participation and passive listening. If children are losing interest, do something active.

◉ **Exaggerate positive behaviors** you want to reinforce. Make a point of using *please* and *thank you*. Look at the child who is talking instead of the child who is interrupting and say, *I am listening to Jerome now.*

◉ **Respond proactively to behavior problems.** Seat children who have trouble attending next to good listeners or your aide. Before circle time, talk to the child about your expectations for behavior and reinforce his or her ability to meet them.

◉ **Make eye contact** with children. Your eyes are probably the strongest management tool you have!

◉ **Practice, practice, practice** whatever you want to do with children BEFORE you come to circle time. This will allow you to be relaxed and have close contact with children, rather than focusing solely on the materials.

◉ **Be ready to go.** Collect all materials before children arrive (waiting time creates chaos!).

◉ **Encourage children to talk**. Be sure you're not talking more than they are!

◉ **Acknowledge the rights** of every member of the group.

◉ **Use a consistent place and time** so children know what to expect.

◉ **Be flexible!** If children are not "with you," then it is time to end the session. Be sure to find a positive ending and closure for the group. (Don't stop the circle as "punishment" for their inability to listen. Just quickly find a good way to end things and move on to the next activity.)

◉ **Use clear and simple directions** so children know what you expect of them at circle time.

◉ **Be dramatic**, change your voice, whisper, make obvious mistakes, use riddles, be humorous, but most of all…involve the children!

◉ **Ask open-ended questions.** *What would happen if____? What do you think about ____? What do you imagine? How many ways can you____?*

◉ **Watch for "invisible" or isolated children**. They will need your extra attention at circle time. Be sure to deliberately involve them as much as possible.

◉ **If all else fails, read a good book**! Literature captivates children in ways that nothing else can.

Family Communication

The family is a key ingredient to the success of your program because it is the family that supports the learning the child brings home. Make a point of connecting in a variety of ways, from phone calls to letters or notes sent home. (See page 9 for a sample family letter.) If possible, use e-mail for instant family communication! The family will appreciate your efforts and be more likely to participate actively in your program.

Start the year off right by connecting with families:

- Before school starts, send a letter introducing yourself, and consider including an activity they can do with their child.

- Invite them to collect family pictures for the child to share at school.

- Encourage family members to visit circle time to share a craft, skill, or interest. Ask them to come to read a favorite children's book from their childhood, or a current favorite.

- Invite families to come and talk about their own early school experiences—and bring photos if possible!

- Make a booklet and a tape of circle-time songs to send home for family sing-alongs.

- Establish a brief end-of-the-day circle time to review the events of the day. This will help children remember the day and have something to tell families when they ask, "What did you do in school today?"

Remember, families come in all sorts of configurations. When contacting families, make general invitations for connection and visits, and be open to the diversity of contact you receive. Instead of having a Moms' Day or a Dads' Day, have a Family Day. Be sensitive to changes in children's families by providing a safe place for them to share emotions, fears, and celebrations. If you acknowledge the rich legacy of each child's family, you will be creating a circle time whose dimensions are much greater than the shape of the carpet that defines it.

QUICK ATTENTION GETTERS

- Whisper directions or "mouth the words"!

- Exaggerate whatever children are doing (such as moving around or talking all at once) until they stop and look at you.

- Use a prop—a puppet, a flower, a movement—anything visual to get them to look at you.

- Be silent and smile!

Dear Families,

It's almost that time! It is so exciting to imagine all the children gathering together in our classroom for the first time.

Circle time is an important part of our program. It is the time each day when children meet as a group and learn how to listen, share, and collaborate with others. As you well know, that is not always an easy thing for young children! From time to time throughout the year, you will receive a note asking for help with show and tell or other circle-time assignments. These activities are important to children, and your help and participation are essential to making it all work. Please read the notes that are sent home and make a point of working with your child to do the requested activity.

Family photos are one of the most cherished links children have with you while in school. They are also prized possessions that are hard to let out of the house! Rest assured that any photos you send in will be handled with respect and care and will be returned in the same condition in which they were sent.

We want to meet you at circle time one day. If you have a skill, craft, art, or interest you would like to share with the group, please contact us. Come read a book or sing a song with us. The more we learn about you and your family, the more we can learn about and connect with your child.

This is going to be an amazing year. Thanks for your part in making it great for your child—and all of us!

Sincerely,

Creating Your Circle-Time Area

⊚ Choose an area that is well defined and protected, away from distractions or noise. (For instance, circle time right next to the block area is probably not a good choice!)

⊚ Use visual cues to define the space in which children will sit (carpet squares, place mats, masking-tape lines, or shapes, pillows, or mats).

⊚ Place an easel with chart paper in the area and keep a box of markers nearby.

⊚ Find a drum or other musical instrument that can be used as a signal to call children to circle time or to get their attention. Change it periodically.

⊚ Create a comfortable seat for yourself (slightly raised above the children). This allows them to see what you are showing or reading.

Using This Book

Here's what you'll find on each page:

Materials List
Many of the activities in this book require no materials at all; when they do, they're listed here.

How-To
Simple step-by-step instructions let you know how to make the activity happen.

Skills
This list tells you which skills you're developing during your circle time.

Tips
You'll find plenty of ways to simplify, extend, or enrich the activity.

Songs and Rhymes
Often a song sung to a familiar tune is included. You can copy it onto sentence strips and use a pocket chart to teach children the song, or simply sing it through several times until children are familiar with it.

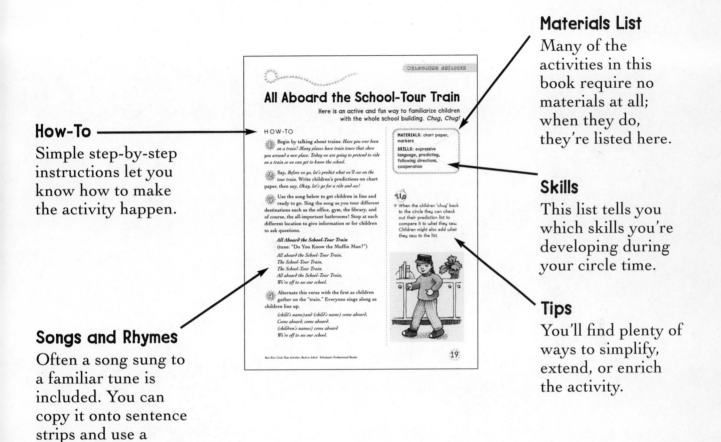

Hi Ho, Hi Ho!

Take the old favorite from "Snow White" and turn it into a "march to meeting time" song. Children will follow you to circle in no time!

MATERIALS: chart paper, markers

SKILLS: following directions, understanding routines, creative movement

HOW-TO

 1 When it is time to gather children, sing this version of the classic song.

Hi Ho, Hi Ho

Hi ho, hi ho,
It's off to school we go.
With a hop in our step
And a great big clap,
Hi ho, hi ho,
Hi ho, hi ho.

(Repeat until children are gathered.)

2 Begin marching around the room, "picking up" children in a line behind you, until all children are marching to your circle-time area.

3 When children arrive at circle, add a quiet verse to settle them down. Put your fingers to your lips as you whisper this last verse:

Hi ho, hi ho,
It's time to sit down slow.
With a quiet clap
Put your hands in your lap
Hi ho, hi ho.

 Tip

● Once you get to circle, you might discuss the different ways children came to school: *Who walked or rode with a parent? Who rode a bus? Did anyone ride a bike?* Write the different modes of travel on chart paper and sing to the tune of "This Is the Way We Wash Our Clothes":

This is the way
we go to school
Go to school, go to school
This is the way
we go to school
So early in the morning.

Use the children's names and their mode of transportation in the song. They can get up and pretend to travel that way around the circle as others sing! For instance:

Joe and Sarah ride a bike
(or walk to school, ride a
car/bus)
Ride a bike, ride a bike
Joe and Sarah ride a bike
On their way to school!

A Piece of the Puzzle

Help your new students see that they are all "a piece of the puzzle." Without each individual child, the class is incomplete!

HOW-TO

1 Mail puzzle pieces out to children before school starts. You might remind families to have children bring the puzzle piece by calling them the night before school starts. (This also gives you an opportunity to tell the children how excited you are to see them tomorrow at school!)

2 As children gather for circle time with their puzzle pieces, sing a song and invite them to place their pieces in the center of the circle:

> **We Are All a Puzzle Piece**
> (tune: "Muffin Man")
>
> *We are all a puzzle piece*
> *A puzzle piece, a puzzle piece.*
> *We are all a puzzle piece*
> *In our happy class.*
>
> *Can you find where it goes*
> *Where it goes, where it goes?*
> *Can you find where it goes?*
> *To place it is our task.*

3 Invite children to notice which pieces are "edge pieces" and have them begin putting the puzzle together as a group, starting on the edges and working toward the middle.

4 Admire the "group jigsaw" and explain to children that each of them is unique and an important part of the group—just like each puzzle piece.

MATERIALS: a large paper floor puzzle (one piece per child)

SKILLS: social interaction, taking turns, fine motor coordination, memory

- Leave the pieces in the block center or reading corner for children to put together again and again.

One Child, Two Children

Here is a fast-paced game for learning names, using the traditional "One Potato, Two Potato" chant.

HOW-TO

1 Teach children the chant below. Explain that when the rhyme stops on the word *more*, whoever is holding the potato says his or her name!

2 First, demonstrate passing the potato, having the chant end with you so you can show how to say your name. Then, begin the chant and start passing!

> *One child, two children*
> *Three children, four*
> *Five children, six children*
> *Seven children, MORE!*
> *[child's name]!*

3 Repeat the chant enough times so that children hear everyone's name.

MATERIALS: one large raw potato

SKILLS: name recognition, expressive language, fine motor coordination

◉ Play the game frequently so that children can begin to name the child with whom the potato lands. Children will say their new friends' names with gusto!

◉ Play a similar name game: the Hot Potato Game. Show the potato and explain that the object of the game is to pass the potato around the circle as fast as possible while music is playing. When the music stops, the person holding the potato says his name or the others say it for him!

With a Ha-Ha Here...

Old MacDonald may have had a farm, but you'll have a very vocal class! Use this version of the familiar tune to introduce children and help them learn one another's names.

HOW-TO

1 Sing a few verses of the old favorite "Old MacDonald Had a Farm." Encourage children to suggest different sounds for the various animals.

2 Invite children to sing the song in a new way: *How would you like to turn it into a song about our class? Who is the "farmer" or leader in our class? Let's make up new words using my name as the farmer. Then we can use the verses to name each child in the class, and have them make up sounds.*

Ms. Teacher Has a Class
(tune: "Old MacDonald Had a Farm")

(teacher's name) has a class
E-I-E-I-O
And in this class she has a (child's name)
E-I-E-I-O

With a (child provides a sound, such as "ha ha!")
Here a (sound)
There a (sound)
Everywhere a (sound-sound)
(teacher's name) has a class
E-I-E-I-O!

MATERIALS: none

SKILLS: self-esteem, verbal expression, cooperation, name recognition

- Use the *ha-ha* sound if children are too shy to make up a sound! That will get them laughing and maybe even get them to suggest some new sounds.

- Children might practice making up sounds for the song BEFORE you sing it together. This gives children time to think of a sound without feeling "put on the spot" in the middle of the song.

Great Expectations

What do you think children expect from school this year?
Why not ask them?

HOW-TO

1 Toward the end of the first week of school, children will probably talk more freely in the circle. Encourage them to imagine what will happen this year by asking, *What do you think we will do in school this year?*

2 Write each child's suggestion on chart paper, along with his or her name. (Invite children to say each child's name to reinforce name recognition.) *Brandon says he thinks he will build tall towers with blocks this year. This is how Brandon's name is written.*

3 To prompt more discussion, ask, *What do you expect to learn to do this year that you didn't know how to do last year?* Record children's ideas and title the list "Great Expectations." Hang it in the hall for families to read.

MATERIALS: chart paper, markers

SKILLS: name recognition, expressive language, predicting, creative thinking, problem solving

 TIPS

◉ Remember to accept all children's ideas equally, without criticism or comparison. This is an important time for children to learn that they can express an idea without fear of being wrong.

◉ Save the "Great Expectations" chart for comparison at the end of the year. Then ask, *Did we learn these things? What else did we learn?*

Meet New Friends

The first step to getting children to feel comfortable in the group is to have them learn one another's names. Use this simple song to break the ice!

HOW-TO

1 Ask children, *How do you say hello? Can you say it with your face, with your voice, with your hands? How many ways can you say hello?* Try all the different ways children suggest.

2 Explain, *You can also say hello with a song.* Teach children this simple greeting song that incorporates their names. Sing the song through first using your name and the name of a child. Demonstrate how to shake hands at the end!

> **Meet New Friends**
> (tune: "Make New Friends")
>
> *Meet new friends,*
> *At circle time.*
> *This is (teacher's name),*
> *And this is (child's name).*

3 Ask: *What do you say when you are introduced to someone? You say, "Hello, how are you?"* Add a second verse as they shake hands.

> *Hello friend*
> *And how are you?*
> *I am happy (or any other adjective)*
> *And I am too!*

MATERIALS: none

SKILLS: name recognition, self-esteem, manners

TIP

◉ Make a list of ways to say hello in different languages.

All Aboard the School-Tour Train

Here is an active and fun way to familiarize children with the whole school building. *Chug, Chug!*

HOW-TO

1 Begin by talking about trains: *Have you ever been on a train? Many places have train tours that show you around a new place. Today we are going to pretend to ride on a train so we can get to know the school.*

2 Say, *Before we go, let's predict what we'll see on the tour train.* Write children's predictions on chart paper, then say, *Okay, let's go for a ride and see!*

3 Use the song below to get children in line and ready to go. Sing the song as you tour different destinations such as the office, gym, the library, and of course, the all-important bathrooms! Stop at each different location to give information or for children to ask questions.

> **All Aboard the School-Tour Train**
> (tune: "Do You Know the Muffin Man?")
>
> *All aboard the School-Tour Train,*
> *The School-Tour Train,*
> *The School-Tour Train.*
> *All aboard the School-Tour Train,*
> *We're off to see our school.*

4 Alternate this verse with the first as children gather on the "train." Everyone sings along as children line up.

> *(child's name) and (child's name) come aboard,*
> *Come aboard, come aboard.*
> *(children's names) come aboard*
> *We're off to see our school.*

MATERIALS: chart paper, markers

SKILLS: expressive language, predicting, following directions, cooperation

◉ When the children "chug" back to the circle they can check out their prediction list to compare it to what they saw. Children might also add what they saw to the list.

Who Am I?

Here is a simple and heartwarming activity to help children feel part of the group. Save this until the end of the second week!

HOW-TO

1 Tell children, *We are going to play a guessing game with all of our new friends. Are you ready?* Invite a child to reach in the bag and pull out a picture. Ask, *Who am I?* The child says the classmate's name or points to that child.

2 Encourage the child in the photo to talk about what is happening in the picture. If the pictures are from the classroom, ask the children to name where the picture was taken and what part of the class day it was.

3 That child picks a photo next.

MATERIALS: photos of each child (children can bring them from home, or you can use an instant camera in class), a colorful bag

SKILLS: visual discrimination and memory, expressive language

● Reverse the game and give a clue about one child (*she has red hair, her name begins with S...*), then invite children to guess who it is. Show children the photo to check their answers!

Classroom Treasure Hunt

During the first weeks of school, children become familiar with their environment. This activity sends children on a treasure hunt all over the room for a special surprise.

HOW-TO

1 Use a bit of drama to introduce the treasure hunt! Hide the first clue in a book that you plan to share and act startled when you find the envelope inside: *What is this? It looks like a message. Should we read what it says?*

2 Read the message and ask children if they can guess where the clue is telling them to look. As a class, choose the most likely place and go check it out.

3 Each clue takes the children to a different part of the room. At each destination, invite children to notice what is in the area so that they familiarize themselves with each part of the room.

4 Keep hunting until you get to the treasure! (Hide it in the circle-time area so that everyone can enjoy the surprise together.)

MATERIALS: envelopes with treasure-hunt clues, a special snack

In advance, write out about six simple treasure-hunt clues such as *"Look inside the box of a candy game"* (hidden in a Candyland game) or *"Go to the place where towers are built and look around the corner"* (hidden around the corner of a block shelf).

SKILLS: visual discrimination, listening, deduction

- If you have a large group, send a few different children to look each time. This will prevent crowding, and it allows others to be cheerleaders!

- Play the treasure-hunt game whenever you want to introduce a new toy or material to a center. (Clues should lead children to that particular center.)

Our Special Friends

Children often feel more relaxed in a new setting if they have a familiar comfort object with them. Have a circle-time gathering of these special friends!

HOW-TO

1 Ask children to bring their special friend to circle time. Sing a song to gather children for this special meeting:

> **Come and Meet Our Special Friends**
> (tune: "Mary Had a Little Lamb")
>
> *Come and meet our special friends,*
>   *special friends, special friends.*
> *Come and meet our special friends,*
> *That we brought from home!*

2 Invite each child to introduce his or her special friend to the group, holding it up for others to see.

3 Make a "Special Friends" chart with children's names and the names of their special friends. Examine the chart together, looking for any similar names, words, or letters. Children can share other information about their friend.

4 At the end of circle time, send children off with a song and a purpose. Encourage them to find an area of the room they would like to show to their friend, and sing this additional verse to the song as they explore.

> *We will show our special friends,*
>   *special friends, special friends*
> *We will show our special friends*
> *All around the room!*

MATERIALS: children's favorite stuffed animal or doll, chart paper, markers

In advance, write a note home inviting children to bring in a stuffed animal or doll. Explain that there will be a special day to meet and celebrate these friends.

SKILLS: sharing, social interaction, letter recognition

Tips

- If available, use a camera to take pictures of children with their friends. Put these in the writing center where children can draw and write about the day they shared at school!

- Be prepared with an attractive collection of stuffed animals for children to use in case they forget theirs or don't have one to use.

Sharing Feelings

For some children, this is the first experience away from home.
Instead of avoiding the topic, talk about it!

HOW-TO

1 Start the activity with a book that will get children thinking and talking about feelings. Ask questions to elicit conversation about separation: *How did the character feel about going to school? What did he feel like when he got there? How did he feel at the end of the day?*

2 After discussing the book, invite children to talk about how they feel: *Were you worried about coming to school? How did you feel about leaving your family?* Make the time and space available for children to talk if they want. You can start the conversation by telling where your family is when you are in school, such as: *My son is in high school and my husband is building a house today. What is your family doing while you are here? Where do you think they are now?* It sounds simple, but it is a very effective way to help children deal with separation anxiety!

MATERIALS: your favorite children's books about starting school

SKILLS: expressive language, sharing, cooperation

 TIPS

⊙ Instead of using books to introduce the conversation, try telling the story of *your* first day of school! Children will be fascinated to hear that you had a similar experience— and that you were little once! If possible, bring a picture of yourself when you were their age.

⊙ Model good listening skills. Remember to make eye contact with the child speaking and to not let others interrupt. If they do, give a gentle reminder as you continue to look at the child speaking.

⊙ Invite families to send in pictures of themselves at work for children to share with the group.

Passport for Play

Introduce children to the fun of center time as children use "passports" to navigate the room.

HOW-TO

1 Introduce the passports to the group. If possible, show children your own real passport and explain how and why it is used. (Be sensitive to the situations of children whose families are newcomers to the United States, since they may be in different phases of the immigration process.)

2 Hold up one passport at a time and ask children to say whose it is.

3 Show the stickers or rubber stamps that you will have in various areas of the room and demonstrate how children should put one sticker or stamp on the page when they are finished playing in that area.

4 At the end of the week, have children share their passports at circle time. Invite children to notice which areas they visited most often: *Is everybody's passport marked the same? Did everyone go to the same places this week? Why or why not?*

MATERIALS: "passports" for each child, a collection of stickers or rubber stamps

To make passports, take four or five sheets of paper, fold, and staple. Add each child's name to the cover and label each page with the name of a different center of the room.

SKILLS: following directions, name recognition, inference

● Send passports home to families to help them see what their child enjoys doing in school.

● You can have a child in each center be in charge of stamping the passports, or set up a passport center in the circle-time area during activity time!

The Teacher in the Dell

Use the familiar song "The Farmer in the Dell"
to help children practice one another's names.

HOW-TO

1 Sing one verse of "The Farmer in the Dell." Tell children there is a circle game that goes with the song.

2 Sing the song through one time before you play the game:

(teacher's name) has a class.
(teacher's name) has a class.
Hi Ho Dee Derrio
(teacher's name) has a class!

3 Have children form a circle, hold hands, and walk around the circle singing the verse.

4 Introduce the game and new verses. Tell children you are going to sing the song a little differently, and the trick to the game is listening for their name!

5 Stand in the center of the circle and sing:

(teacher's name) takes Danny (name of child),
(teacher's name) takes Danny
Hi Ho Dee Derrio
(teacher's name) takes Danny.

6 As each child is added to the center of the circle, that child names another friend and brings him or her in.

Danny takes Jennifer (name of a second child)
Danny takes Jennifer
Hi Ho Dee Derrio
Danny takes Jennifer!

MATERIALS: none

SKILLS: name recognition, self-esteem, cooperation

- At first, children may be unsure of other children's names. They might just tap the friend they want to bring in. The more you play, the better children will become at remembering names—and they'll definitely be more comfortable choosing a friend!

- Make name tags for children to wear during the song.

- Continue until everyone is together in the center, singing the final verse!

We are a happy class,
We are a happy class.
Heigh Ho Dee Derrio
We are a happy class!

Duck, Duck, YOU!

Practice each other's names with a fast-moving game!

HOW-TO

1 Play the familiar game of duck, duck, goose. Then, explain that you're going to play a variation of the game, in which the child who is "it" walks around the circle and says "duck" as she lightly taps the head of each child. But when she gets to someone whose name she knows, she touches his head and says his name, and begins to run around the circle as that child gets up and chases after her.

2 The child who is "it" tries to get back to the open space where the child she has tapped had been sitting—before the tapped child "tags" her.

3 The child left standing is now "it." Repeat until each child has been chosen!

MATERIALS: none

SKILLS: name recognition, memory, gross motor skills

- Make sure each child has a turn to be "tapped." If children don't know each other's names, whisper a name to the child who is "it."

Who Says?

Play a version of Simon Says in which everybody wins! Children will enjoy leading this game—and teaching their name to the group.

HOW-TO

1 Have children wear their name necklaces. Introduce the game by asking, *Who can tell me how to play Simon Says?* Explain that they are going to play a new version, in which the leader uses her or his name instead of *Simon*. For instance, if Rhonda is the leader, she would say: *Rhonda says touch your toes. Rhonda says wiggle your nose.*

2 Remind children the special nature of this no-lose game by saying: *The best part of the game is that nobody is ever left out because the leader only gives directions using her name!* Play the drum or other instrument to signal when it's time for the next leader to play.

> **MATERIALS:** drum or other instrument
>
> **SKILLS:** name recognition, listening, following directions

⦿ If children seem to choose the same commands repeatedly, give them a few words of inspiration! You might suggest they make a low or a high movement, a hand or a leg movement, even a silly face!

ABC Name Graph

Here's a fun way for children to learn one another's names—
by their first letters!

HOW-TO

① Ask, *Do you know which letter your name starts with?* Pass out the name cards and invite children to compare the letters in their names with those of the children sitting next to them in the circle. Prompt them with: *How are your names the same or different? Do you notice any names that start with the same letter?*

② Show the alphabet graph chart. Start at the top with the letter *A*, and ask, *Does anyone's name start with this letter?* Children can refer to their name cards. Use self-sticking adhesive to put name cards next to each letter. Keep adding name cards until all the children's names are graphed.

③ Examine the alphabet graph together, and ask: *Which letter has the most names? Which letter has the least? Are there any letters that have no names?*

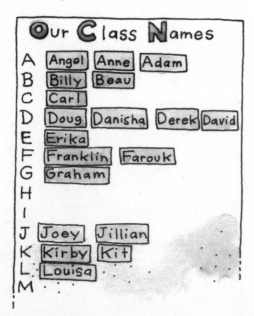

MATERIALS: chart paper with the letters A–Z written vertically down the left side, self-sticking adhesive, name card for each child

SKILLS: letter and name recognition, phonemic awareness, matching

● Put the names that start with the same letter into a song:

The Alphabet Name Song
(tune: "Here We Go 'Round the Mulberry Bush")

*Here are our names that start with A
Start with A, start with A
Ann and Amy start with A
Let's play again!*

● Use the alphabet chart throughout the year. Children can find other words that start with a particular letter and add them to the graph. You might also use pictures of things that start with a particular letter.

Punchinello

Punchinello is a puppet that loves to mimic! He's also great for leading this fun, getting-to-know-you game. Play this once children are more comfortable doing something in front of the group.

HOW-TO

1 Introduce Punchinello and demonstrate how he likes to play follow-the-leader games (make him perform a simple motion for the others to copy).

2 Present the song by singing (or chanting) it through a few times to the traditional tune and demonstrating with the puppet what the leader should do. Children can follow along and make the same movements as the puppet does.

See who is here
Punchinello, Punchinello
See who is here
Punchinello, funny you!

What can you do?
Punchinello, Punchinello
We can do it too
Punchinello, funny you!

3 Time to play! Ask: *Would you like to be Punchinello? Here is a hat like his for you to wear while you are the leader.* One child puts on the hat, sits in the center of the circle, leads the song, and makes a motion for others to copy.

4 At the end of the song, the child in the center closes his or her eyes and spins around the circle, with one hand pointing to pick the next Punchinello. (Of course, any child is free to say "no, thank you" if he or she is not ready!)

MATERIALS: puppet wearing a paper hat, a child-size paper hat

SKILLS: name recognition, expressive language, creative movement, following directions, taking turns

- Replace the name "Punchinello" in the song with the children's names. You might want to use both first and last names to match the correct number of beats in the song. For example:

See who is here
Liz Gordon, Liz Gordon
See who is here
Liz Gordon funny YOU!

- After circle time, children can make personalized paper hats with their names, using favorite decorations. Use these the next time you play Punchinello!

Birthday Chart

Almost every classroom has a birthday chart!
Why not create one together at circle time?

HOW-TO

1. Talk about birthdays, asking: *What do you do at a birthday party? Do you know when your birthday is?* Bring out the bags and explain that each represents a month of the year.

2. Spread the tablecloth in the center of the circle and say, *We are going to have a pretend birthday party to help us learn when one another's birthdays are.* Request that a volunteer empty the first bag as children watch to see whose names fall out with the confetti! Those children then use self-sealing adhesive to attach their names to the birthday chart.

3. Continue until the bags are emptied and all the names are on the chart. Ask, *Which month has the most birthdays?*

4. Celebrate by singing a new birthday song to everybody, to the tune of "Twinkle, Twinkle Little Star":

   Happy birthday to new friends
   We can't wait to celebrate
   Happy birthday to new friends
   Birthday time is really great!

MATERIALS: 12 birthday party bags (one for each month of the year) filled with confetti and index cards with the names of children whose birthday is in that month, large sheet or tablecloth, decorative birthday poster with each month listed and room for names underneath, self-sealing adhesive

SKILLS: name recognition, sorting, cooperation, sharing

⊙ When it's time to line up, invite children to leave the circle when their month is called! Call out months in order.

Who's Missing?

Once everyone knows their classmates' names, they can notice who is not in school on any given day!

HOW-TO

1 Tell children how proud you are that they are learning one another's names! Explain that this game will let them show off just how well they know them.

2 Children close their eyes while you cover one volunteer with the blanket.

3 Children then open their eyes and name the child who they think is under the blanket.

4 Repeat. In the next round, the child who was hiding can help you cover the next child.

MATERIALS: blanket or sheet

SKILLS: cooperation, memory, name recognition, self-esteem

- If children are nervous about going under the blanket, try being the first one to hide.

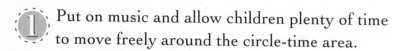

Find a Friendly Face

What's better than finding a friend? Finding a friend and making something fun together!

HOW-TO

1 Put on music and allow children plenty of time to move freely around the circle-time area.

2 Stop the music and tell children to freeze. Say, *I am going to pass out half a funny-face picture to each of you. Don't show it to anyone. When the music starts you can move around again but when the music stops, find a friend near you and show each other your half-faces.*

3 Start the music and watch children move with their pictures. Without them noticing, stop the music and call out, "Freeze!" Children should find a friend, and they should show each other their half-faces, then put them together to make a new face. (Explain that right sides should match with left sides.)

4 Be prepared for peals of laughter as children admire the face they have created together! Ask, *Can you give your new friend a name? Two at a time, hold up your face cards together and shout out your friend's name.*

MATERIALS: lively movement music, same-size magazine pictures of faces (cut in half lengthwise, enough for each child to have half a face)

SKILLS: social interaction, creative movement, expressive language

Tips

◉ Put the face cards in a learning center. Children will enjoy making many different face combinations. They can also practice writing the name of the new friend and telling something about him or her.

◉ If you are teaching colors or shapes, you can make sets of cards with matching colors or shapes. The object of the game then becomes to find who has the matching card.

◉ Cut the center out of sturdy paper plates and tape red, yellow, or blue cellophane or tissue paper over each hole. When the music stops, children find a friend, put their plates together, and hold them up to the light to create a new color.

Circle-Time Buddies

As children become more familiar with each other's names, continue playing community-building games.

HOW-TO

1 Hand out cards and ask children to keep them private. Tell them they will hold the card while moving around, and save its surprise for the end of the game!

2 Start the music and invite children to walk around the room and greet each other by name: "Good morning,_____" or "Hello,_____." Children might enjoy shaking hands when they meet. Demonstrate this with one child, stressing the friendly greeting.

3 Continue the game until it seems that everyone has been greeted. Stop the music and say, "Freeze!" Ask children to turn their cards around (the rest of their body remains "frozen"). Everyone looks around for their match; when they find one, they sit down together in the circle. They are circle-time buddies for the day!

MATERIALS: sets of matching shape, color, or letter cards (enough pairs for each child to have a match in the group), quiet instrumental music

SKILLS: cooperation, visual discrimination, manners

⊙ This game can be used to form pairs for other activities, or for lining up.

⊙ Change the images on the cards to represent any subject you are studying. For instance, during your dinosaur unit, have dinosaur pairs for children to match!

Best-Ever Circle Time Activities: Back to School Scholastic Professional Books

I Am a Poem!

Celebrate children's identities as individuals and as group members by creating poetry together. Try creating one or two of these poems each week in September!

HOW-TO

1 Model writing an "I Am…" poem by writing one about yourself, with the group's help. The format for the poem is a repeating line that starts with "I am…." Each line describes something about the person, his or her name or nicknames, feelings, and interests. Encourage children to add ideas to your poem.

2 Ask for a child to volunteer to make up an "I Am…" poem. Use photos of each child for inspiration.

3 As children suggest lines for the poem, write their words on chart paper. You can help them by asking questions. You might ask, *What is the name you are called at home? Are you a sister or a brother? Are you big or little? How old are you? How do you feel today?*

I am George.
I am George Smith.
I am Smitty.
I am brother.
I am big
I am five years old.
I am fun to play with.
I am happy today!

MATERIALS: chart paper, markers, crayons, photo of each child

SKILLS: name recognition, creative language, speaking and dictating

⊙ Collect the poems in a big class book. Children can add self-portraits to their page as illustration.

⊙ Read children's poems occasionally at circle time. The repetitive nature of the wording makes this a quick and easy reading exercise. Children will learn to read the sight words *I* and *am* very quickly!

Follow My Move!

Here's a new twist on follow-the-leader—add music and make it a movement game! Children take turns being leader or followers.

HOW-TO

1 Start the game by playing a quick version of traditional follow-the-leader (with you as the leader). Do simple motions that children can follow as they sit in the circle. Then, explain that there is a different way to play the game: *In this game, the leader dances around!*

2 Introduce the leader hat. Explain that whoever is wearing the hat is the leader and the rest of the children must follow the leader around, doing whatever he or she does!

3 Have everyone stand up and find a comfortable space in the circle where they will not bump into anyone. Start the music and off you go!

4 When the music stops, pass the leader hat to someone else and start again!

MATERIALS: a variety of energetic music, a hat for the leader

SKILLS: following directions, observing, listening, social interaction, cooperation

- Play this outside on a nice day. In follow-the-leader tag, the leader makes a movement that others copy. But at the same time, he or she is trying to tag someone. The child tagged becomes the next leader!

Best-Ever Circle Time Activities: Back to School Scholastic Professional Books

Meet the Family

Now that everyone's getting to know one another, it's time for children to meet their classmates' families. In this activity, children use family photos to introduce their loved ones.

HOW-TO

1 Start by introducing your own family photos. (Children are very curious to know more about your life outside of school!) Take time to share your photos one at a time, and invite children to ask questions about the photos.

2 Have the children who are sharing their photos sit near you. Invite one child to begin sharing. You might ask questions: *Who is in the picture? What is she doing? Where was this picture taken?*

3 Encourage other children to ask questions, too. Ask them, *What would you like to know about this family? What do you notice in the photos that you'd like to ask about?*

4 Use chart paper to record what children share about their family, and post the photos next to the notes for the rest of the day. During the day, children might talk with others about the photos and their family in more informal ways.

> **MATERIALS:** photos of your family, children's family photos, chart paper, markers
>
> *Ahead of time,* send a letter home asking for family photos (plan on having two or three children show photos each day).
>
> **SKILLS:** name recognition, expressive language and vocabulary, taking turns

⊙ Family photos provide comfortable "touchstones" for children at the beginning of the year. Ask families if you can post the photos inside children's cubbies.

Visiting Readers

What is better than sharing photos of your family?
Sharing the real people! In this activity, family members
share a special circle time.

HOW-TO

1 Set up a weekly family reading circle time. Invite family members to sign up for a day to read to the children (you might help them choose books that are short and visual, and encourage them to practice reading it before they come).

2 Prepare children for the visitor. Talk about appropriate manners: *How do we greet a visitor? What can we do to make them comfortable?* Have children practice greetings with one another before the visitor comes.

3 Ask children to think about questions to ask the visitor when he or she comes. Write them on chart paper for easy reference during the visit. (Sometimes, with the excitement of the visitor's arrival, children forget what they wanted to ask or say!)

4 When the family reader arrives for circle time, have his or her child and a few friends show him or her where to sit and what to do. (Children love showing what they know about their room and being in charge for a change!)

MATERIALS: note posted on door requesting visitors come in and read a book to the group on certain dates (families can bring their own book or choose one in the classroom)

SKILLS: expressive language, listening, name recognition, manners

⊙ Invite children to create a Visiting Reader chair, name tag, or hat. Provide art and collage materials for children to create a fanciful decoration that will identify the visitor. Not only will the children enjoy making it—the reader will love being honored in such a way!

Name That Tune!

One of the best ways to help children feel comfortable is to share what they already know. A great place to start is with familiar songs.

HOW-TO

1 Start a song session! Begin by humming a tune and ask children to guess what it is. Choose simple songs that most children know such as "The Farmer in the Dell" or "Twinkle, Twinkle, Little Star."

2 When children guess what the song is, sing it together! Children are often comforted by singing familiar songs. Write the name of the song on chart paper for children to read.

3 Try another tune for children to guess and sing, and add the title of the song to the chart. Children might also enjoy leading this game.

> **MATERIALS:** chart paper, marker
>
> **SKILLS:** expressive language, listening, singing

 Tip

⦿ Write the words to each song on chart paper and invite children to read and illustrate. Use these at subsequent songfests!

Morning Rituals

A morning movement or song helps mark the beginning of the day.
The ritual gives children a reassuring touchstone activity.

HOW-TO

1 Create a special movement (such as a high five, a secret handshake, or sign language for "hello" or "welcome") to use as children enter the room! The sign-language movement for "hello" is an open hand with a touch of the fingers to the temple like a salute. The sign for "welcome" is a flat open hand with palm up moving from the torso out to the other person and back again. Try combining the two movements to say "hello and welcome"!

2 At circle time, silently "pass" the welcoming gestures around the group to set a focused and quiet tone to the gathering. Start with the child next to you. He or she passes it to the next child and so on until the sign gets back to you.

MATERIALS: none

SKILLS: self-esteem, cooperation, expressive language, fine motor coordination

- Ask children to create a secret handshake or other movement to use to start the meeting!

- Encourage children to make up a cheer or a chant to use as a greeting ritual. Or, use a chant such as:

  Two, four, six, eight, who do we appreciate?
  (child's name, child's name)
  HOORAY!

Best-Ever Circle Time Activities: Back to School Scholastic Professional Books

Signing In

Here's a simple and effective way to take attendance.
As children join the circle, they can put their "best face forward"
by turning their picture tag on the circle-time sign-in board.

HOW-TO

 As children come to the rug, invite them to find their card on the board and turn it over to show their photo.

 Sing a song as children "sign in":

Welcome Children
(tune: "Good Night, Ladies")

Welcome children, welcome children
Welcome children, it's time to turn your tag.
(Repeat)

TIPs

◉ Use the sign-in board as a tool for discussing who is here and who is missing. Ask children to count off around the circle. Practice one-to-one correspondence by comparing that number with the number of faces showing on the board.

◉ Play "Who's Missing?" Invite children to look around and say who is absent from the circle. Check their answers on the board!

MATERIALS: a handmade circle-time sign-in board

Use heavy posterboard as a base. Glue-gun clothespins onto the poster in rows and write children's names above them. Use index cards to create tags for each child, with a photo of the child on one side and a sticker or drawing on the other. Laminate the tags and attach to clothespins so that you cannot see photos.

SKILLS: self-esteem, following directions, fine motor coordination

Dylan

Quiet Hands

Taking turns is one of the most important skills young children can learn. But it doesn't have to be hard work—you can make it a game!

HOW-TO

1 Show children a ball. Explain that it is a "talk" ball: *Whoever is holding the ball can talk, and the rest of us listen.*

2 Show children how to quietly raise their hands if they have something to say. (You might show children how to put one hand in the air and the finger of their other hand over their mouth in the "Shhhhh" sign).

3 Tell children to raise their hands if they want to answer the question you're about to ask. Begin with a simple question, such as, *What is your favorite color?* Roll the ball to a child who has a "quiet hand" raised.

4 The child with the ball answers the question, then rolls the ball back to you. You then roll it to another child who has his or her hand raised. Reinforce and acknowledge the good listening they are doing as one child speaks!

MATERIALS: a soft ball

SKILLS: turn taking, listening, attending, fine motor coordination

- Children can roll the ball to the next child who has his or her hand raised.

- Some good questions to start the year: *What is your full name? What is your favorite food? What did you do last night? What do you want to do this weekend?*

- As you play, sing a song to reinforce the skills of talking and listening:

Take Your Turn
(tune: "Farmer in the Dell")

*I roll the ball to you
It's your turn to talk
You may have
    some things to say,
Let's listen to your thoughts!*

Best-Ever Circle Time Activities: Back to School Scholastic Professional Books

Search Party

Children develop a sense of belonging when they know how to navigate the room. Use this game to acquaint children with the different areas of their environment.

HOW-TO

1 Ask children, *How well do you think you know our room? Let's play a game to see!* Present the bag or box of objects and invite children to take out one object at a time. Ask them to describe the object and its use: *Where do you remember finding this object in the room? Can you find where it belongs?*

2 Choose two or three "searchers." Children can sing this song as the searchers go to the different centers looking for the place where each object is found:

> **Can You Tell Us?**
> (tune: "London Bridge")
>
> *Can you tell us where it's found?*
> *Where it's found, where it's found.*
> *Can you tell us where it's found,*
> *(child's name) and (child's name)?*

MATERIALS: pillowcase (or bag or box) filled with two classroom objects from different centers (blocks, writing, art, puzzles), or pictures cut from school-supply catalogs, showing materials from different centers

SKILLS: visual discrimination, matching, visual memory, turn taking

Tips

- If children are having trouble finding something, you might say, *You're getting warmer/colder* to help them along!

- Reverse the game by giving clues about the object in the bag, and have the children guess what it is: *This is something that is hard on one end and soft on the other. We use it in the art area. What is it? (a paintbrush)* When children guess, they go put it away in the correct center.

Calendar Craze

The calendar is a regular part of circle time,
but why not do something a bit different?
Here are some unique and fun ways to mark off the days.

HOW-TO

1 Show children the posterboard calendar and ask, *What do we use this for?* Show children different types of calendars and discuss their similarities and differences. Explain that in school, you'll use the calendar as a way to mark off the days spent together.

2 Focus on the purpose of the calendar as a way to mark time. Starting with the first box, invite a child to use markers or stickers to fill in the day. Each day, have a child draw or add a sticker to a box to mark the day. By the end of the month, you'll have a very colorful calendar!

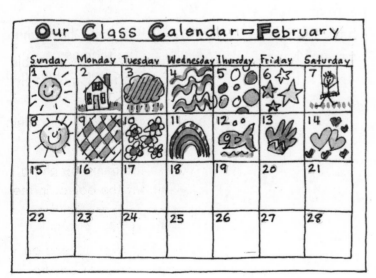

MATERIALS: posterboard divided into rows and columns like a calendar, markers or stickers, different types of calendars

SKILLS: organizing, sequencing, counting, taking turns

- Daily, ask children to count how many days are filled in. Follow up by saying, *That is the number of days we've been in school this month!*

- If there is a special event coming up, mark it on the calendar. Children can also count the number of days until an event occurs by counting the empty squares on the calendar.

- You might also fill in the calendar at closing circle.

My Job, Your Job

Everyone has a job to do in the classroom! Build awareness of the importance of classroom helpers by creating a chart together.

HOW-TO

1 Ask children to tell you what they think your job is as a teacher. Write their ideas on chart paper. You may be surprised to hear what they think!

2 Then ask what they think their job is and record their responses. Display these charts in the room to refer to all year, to remind children of their responsibilities in the classroom.

3 From the list, have children brainstorm another list of responsibilities that can be used to create a Job Chart. Jobs might include watering plants, holding the door, feeding the pets, setting the table, and leading the line.

4 Have children choose pictures to paste on each pie-shaped section of the circular chart. Attach clothespins to name tags, put them in a bag, and have children draw names for the jobs once a week. Clip these on the sections of the chart.

MATERIALS: chart paper, markers, large piece of posterboard cut into a circle, pictures from catalogs or magazines to represent different classroom jobs, bag, clothespins (or Velcro dots), name tags

SKILLS: expressive language, responsibility, cooperation

● Refer to the Job Chart when exploring the themes of neighborhood and community.

Making Our Own Rules

Children are more likely to abide by the rules if they have a hand in creating them. Create a "Circle Time Rules" poster together!

HOW-TO

1 Discuss circle-time rules. Ask children what rules they think are important, and record their thoughts on chart paper.

2 Read them back and choose one to discuss further. Each day, choose another one to discuss until you have several main rules to post in your circle-time area.

MATERIALS: chart and mural paper, markers

SKILLS: cooperation, expressive language, taking turns, listening

● Children can learn the process of voting by taking a vote at the end of all the discussions for the rule they think is most important. Record their votes. Choose the three or four rules with the most votes as the official circle-time rules!

Our Rules

1. Let one child at a time speak.

2. Be safe.

3. Be ready to listen.

4. Come to the circle time rug quietly.

A Time Line of Rules

Use visual reminders to help children remember what to do and when. Photographs enable children to refer to and "read" the rules!

HOW-TO

1 Discuss rules for a typical day: *What rules do we need to remember when we are on the bus? What do we need to do when we arrive at school? What are the rules during activity time? What are the playground rules?*

2 Use the photos to help children organize their thinking about rules. Place the photos in a row, in time order, from left to right on a long strip of mural paper. Ask children to help you think of a title for each event and write this on the time line.

4 Starting with the first photo, ask children to suggest rules for that time (for instance, if the photo is of a child entering the classroom, a rule might be "Walk! Remember not to run."), then write these on the chart.

5 Continue asking children to add rules for each picture. (This project might span several circle-time sittings.)

MATERIALS: mural paper, markers, photos of various daily events

SKILLS: cooperation, expressive language, taking turns, left-to-right progression, listening

In advance, *take photos with a disposable or instant camera of the major events of the day (snack time, circle time, centers, and so on), from start to finish.*

- ◉ Post the time line at children's eye level along the bottom edge of a bulletin board.

- ◉ When problems arise, have children find the time period they are currently in and check to see the rules.

You've Got Mail

Turn your circle-time area into a mini post office! Children will delight in finding mail when they come to circle time—it may encourage children who are a bit reluctant to join in!

HOW-TO

1 Toward the end of September, introduce a mailbox system! (Children will be more familiar with one another's names and faces by now.) Show children the mailbox pockets on the chart and have them find their name and photo. Ask: *Do you have any mail? Let's look and see.*

2 Use a song to organize the collecting of mail:

Who Has Mail?

(tune: "Frere Jacques")

Who has mail, who has mail?
(child's name) and (child's name)!
What is in your mailbox?
What is in your mailbox?
Go and see, you've got mail!

◉ Use the mailboxes to send notes home to parents.

◉ If children want to draw or write to a friend, they simply find his or her picture on the mailbox and copy the name!

◉ Keep paper and writing and drawing supplies near the mailboxes. Children can use them during activity time to write messages and draw pictures for their classmates.

◉ Don't forget to make a mailbox for yourself!

> **MATERIALS:** hanging shoe bag with pockets (or a posterboard with self-sealing bags attached), a name card with a photo for each child (glued on the pocket or bag), paper, stickers, crayons, markers
>
> **SKILLS:** self-esteem, visual discrimination, pre-reading and -writing
>
> *In advance,* place a short note in each child's mailbox. Use mostly drawings or simple words to state your message.

What Doesn't Belong?

Now that children are more familiar with their classmates and the classroom routines, they can play this fun guessing game.

HOW-TO

1 Fill the tray with objects from one area of the room, plus one object that in some way doesn't belong in the group. Cover the tray and place it on the floor in the center of the circle.

2 Explain how to play the guessing game: *Hidden under here are some objects that are all from one area of our room, except for one object that doesn't belong. When I take the cover off, raise your hand if you think you know which area of the room the objects are from.*

3 After children have guessed the name of the area the objects come from, ask, *Who can guess which object doesn't belong with these things? Why doesn't it belong?* Discuss the name of each object and how it is used, then ask where the odd object belongs.

4 Cover the tray again and refill it with objects from another area of the room.

MATERIALS: tray, small blanket or tablecloth, toys, manipulatives, tools and other objects from the various areas of the classroom (different shapes of blocks, small cars, toy people)

SKILLS: visual discrimination, memory, expressive language, inference, deduction

- Play the game whenever you are introducing a new material to a learning center. You will be introducing the material, its use, and its place in the classroom.

- Put two objects that don't belong in the group and see if children notice!

- Reverse the game. Show a tray full of classroom objects first. Then cover it and secretly take one object away. Ask: *What is missing?*

Play Passes

Organizing the day often starts at circle time, when children make choices about which learning centers they want to visit. Use this simple, child-tested system for managing each learning center.

HOW-TO

1 Introduce the Play Passes by starting a discussion about crowding, asking, *Have you ever been in a crowd?* Then ask children what might happen if all of them wanted to play in the blocks area at the same time: *How would it feel? Would you be happy there? What can we do?*

2 Ask children to suggest the number of children they think might comfortably play in a particular area.

3 Show the Play Passes. Explain how adults use similar things at big events. Have children examine the different passes and guess which areas the passes are for. Tell children that a pass will allow them to play in a particular area. Bring the passes to the circle every morning and distribute them at the end of circle time.

⦿ When children are finished in a center, they hang the pass on a hook or a chair in the area. This signals to other children that there is now room for someone to play there. This is a simple, self-regulating system.

MATERIALS: "passes" for each learning center (enough for the number of children allowed in each center at a time)

In advance, make "passes" that allow children to play in a particular center. Cut pictures from catalogs or draw pictures representing each learning center (for instance, if five children can play at the block center, make five passes with pictures of blocks on them), glue to tags, and laminate. Punch a hole at the top and string with elastic cord or thick yarn to create necklaces.

SKILLS: cooperation, taking turns, sharing

I Know the Routine!

Children can show how well they know their environment by showing a new friend around!

HOW-TO

1 Hide the puppet in the pillowcase. Introduce it at circle time with a sense of mystery: *I have a new member of our class to introduce to you today. But she is very shy and a bit frightened about coming to school. Do you remember how you felt when you first came to our class? Can you help her feel comfortable?*

2 Once you have elicited children's support, slowly take the puppet out of the pillowcase and introduce her! Invite children to introduce themselves around the circle one by one. Keep things dramatic by whispering to the puppet or making it move or react now and then.

3 Ask children to tell the puppet about their day: *Can you tell our new friend what we do at circle time? What do we do after circle time?*

4 Ask a few children to be in charge of showing the puppet around the room for the day. Say: *Do you think you could help her feel comfortable and learn how to do things here in our classroom? I bet she would like to play with you today!* Children can take turns throughout the day showing the puppet around.

MATERIALS: puppet (or soft doll), pillowcase

SKILLS: expressive language, following directions, cooperation, manners

Tips

- At closing circle, have the puppet thank children for all it has learned—and perhaps make plans for tomorrow!

- Take photos throughout the day. Put these together in a "Meet Our New Friend" book.

Circle Bingo

Use old school-supply catalogs to make a simple bingo game to familiarize children with every object in the classroom.

HOW-TO

1 Remind children that the object of Bingo is to match the object that is called with one on their board. If they have it, they cover the square with a marker. When they have three in a row, they call, "BINGO!"

2 Pass out the boards and markers. Encourage children to examine their board, asking, *What do you notice about the pictures on the board?* Explain that this is a special bingo game that has pictures of things they use in the classroom. Ask, *Can you name everything on your board?*

3 Start simply by calling the names of the objects (use the cards you've created). Make the game more difficult by giving clues: *This is something we use at the easel. You use this in the writing center to draw with.*

4 Keep playing until everyone has had a chance to call "BINGO!"

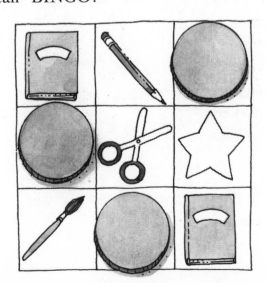

MATERIALS: cardboard bingo grids (three by three) with squares filled with pictures of classroom materials, bingo markers such as dry beans, slips of paper, or plastic chips

You can make four or five different boards and photocopy extras so that every child has one. Make one set of matching cards with the same objects as on the board.

SKILLS: visual discrimination, memory, listening, cooperation

◉ Put the game in a learning center for children to play independently.

A Place for Everyone!

When children know their place in the circle, they naturally feel part of the community. Use a song to remind them how important they are!

HOW-TO

 Sing a song to celebrate everyone's place in the circle:

Our Place in the Circle
(tune: "Sing a Song of Sixpence")

A place for everyone
In our circle time
We are all together
Sharing all the time
Look around the circle
And find a place to sit
These are all your special friends
We make a perfect fit!

 Ask, *How do we know where to find our place in the circle? Would you like to make special seat markers? We can make them here and use them whenever we have circle time.*

 Turn your circle into a collective art area! Pass out the place mats and markers for children to create their own seat marker to use at circle time. Help children write their names on the mat (you might have them trace over your letters written in advance with very thin marker) and use the markers to draw a picture of themselves. This way, their "face" is always in the circle.

Sing the song again, changing the last two lines to:

Find your name and sit right down
We make a perfect fit!

MATERIALS: permanent markers, solid-color plastic place mats

SKILLS: self-esteem, creative expression, name recognition

- Set the mats out before circle time to give children practice finding their names.

- Eventually, setting out the mats can become a job for children to do before circle time, providing great practice in reading names. Children will quickly learn how to read a friend's name if they want to sit near them!

The Cooperation Song

Here's a musical way to remind children of the goals of cooperating and creating a classroom community.

HOW-TO

 1 Start a discussion about cooperation. Write the word on chart paper and add children's dictated definitions of the word. Ask: *What does it mean to cooperate? What do we have to do to cooperate with one another at circle time?*

2 Use this song to illustrate your conversation about cooperation at circle time:

Cooperation
(tune: "Frere Jacques")

Coop-er-a-tion, Coop-er-a-tion
SHARE! CARE! FAIR!
SHARE! CARE! FAIR!
We are all connected,
We are all connected
In our class, in our class.

3 Invite children to add words from their list to replace the second and third lines of the song, and sing it again!

MATERIALS: chart paper, markers

SKILLS: cooperation, collaboration, expressive language, singing

● Sing this whenever you introduce a new cooperation activity or game—it makes a wonderful reminder of how to work together.

Balance Pairs

Cooperative games are great for helping children work together as a community. Here's a physical example of what cooperation can accomplish!

HOW-TO

1 Always start a cooperative game with a short discussion of what it means to cooperate: *When we cooperate, we work together to solve a problem or get things done.*

2 Show the pillows or boxes and ask children to consider how they might work in a pair to carry them from one side of the circle to the other without touching them with their hands.

3 Help children pair off. Give a pillow or box to each pair and invite them to spend a few minutes experimenting with holding it between them—without hands!

4 Put on movement music and ask the pair to start moving toward the large bin or box set up at the other end of the circle. When they get there, they drop it in the box and go back to their original seats.

> **MATERIALS:** movement music, small pillows or boxes, large box or plastic bin
>
> **SKILLS:** balance, creative thinking, gross motor coordination, cooperation

Tips

- Try using balloons instead of pillows or boxes!

- Ask children to suggest what else they can balance between them. Can they balance a paper napkin on top of their heads and move around the circle?

- Bring in a Ping-Pong ball or balloon and ask children how they would move it across the circle without touching it. Or ask: How can we move across the circle without using our feet? How can we move a heavy box of balls across the circle without using our hands?

Collaboration Creation

Use a new version of the classic song "Aiken Drum" to get children working together.

HOW-TO

1 Ask children if they know the song "Aiken Drum." Sing a few bars to help them remember, or teach it to them:

There once was a man who lived in the moon
Lived on the moon, lived on the moon
There once was a man who lived on the moon
And his name was Aiken Drum
And he danced upon a ladle, a ladle, a ladle,
He danced upon a ladle
* and his name was Aiken Drum!*

2 Ask children to think of a different name for the character (it is helpful if the name has three syllables like the original). If they can't think of a name, provide one (such as "Fiddle Fun") to get started.

3 Say: *In the original song, Aiken Drum lives in the moon. Where do you think Fiddle Fun lives? Aiken Drum dances on a ladle. Where does Fiddle Fun dance?* Collect the children's ideas and write out the song. For instance:

Fiddle Fun
(tune: "Aiken Drum")

There once was a man who lived in a box
Lived in a box, lived in a box
There once was a man who lived in a box
And he danced upon a pizza, a pizza, a pizza
He danced upon a pizza and his name was Fiddle Fun!

MATERIALS: chart paper, markers

SKILLS: expressive language, singing, creative thinking, cooperation

⦿ The original song continues describing all the foods Aiken Drum is made of: *His hair is made of spaghetti.* Invite children to sing the song and suggest a different food as you draw a funny picture of the character on the chart paper:

And his head was made of
*   cauliflower,*
*   cauliflower,*
*   cauliflower*
His head was made of
*   cauliflower,*
And his name was
*   Fiddle Fun!*

Blanket Toss

What can a group of young children do with a blanket and a ball? Try these games to find out how many children it takes to keep a ball in the air!

HOW-TO

1. Ask children to describe a time this week that they cooperated with someone: *What did you do? How did it feel?*

2. Bring out the blanket and balls and invite children to think of different ways they could use them in a circle game. (You might start them off by asking them to hold the edges of the blanket as they stand in the circle.)

3. Experiment with the different ideas that children suggest. A great game is to put the ball in the center of the blanket and have children try to bounce it with the blanket (it's not as easy as it sounds)!

4. Try using different-size balls. Ask: *How do they move differently? What would happen if we used more than one ball at a time? Can we roll them from side to side? What happens if we bounce them all?*

MATERIALS: old blanket or sheet, different-size balls

SKILLS: gross motor coordination, sharing, cooperation

- Try a name game in which children move the blanket up and down to create a billowing shape. Then, when the blanket is at its highest point, call two children's names, have them run under it, and let it fall on them! Have them wait until the blanket is billowing again to run back out again, then call two more children and have them do the same thing.

- Go outside and use two blankets and a ball. Create two teams that work together to "throw" the ball from one blanket to the other!

Art by All of Us

With a line here and a line there, children can work together to create a masterpiece of cooperation!

HOW-TO

1 Introduce the activity by asking, *Have you ever seen a drawing made by many different artists? How would that work? How can many people work at the same time without bumping into one another?* Encourage children to talk about the skills that would be needed to create a collaborative picture.

2 Pass out several shapes to each child. Say, *Let's try it with these colored shapes. I will glue one on and when you see a place to put the next piece, raise your hand and I will call you to come up and add it!*

3 One at a time, have children glue a shape to the picture. Encourage children to take a moment to look at the picture and consider where to put the shape before they paste it on. Observation and integration are important parts of collaboration.

4 As children add to the picture, invite the others to suggest what the picture looks like. After the last child has added a shape, the children can work together to create a title for their masterpiece. Ask, *What shall we call our picture?* Write the title on a separate piece of paper and leave room for all the children to sign the work of art.

> **MATERIALS:** chart paper, glue stick, construction-paper shapes in different sizes and colors, crayons or markers
>
> **SKILLS:** cooperation, collaboration, taking turns, creative expression

- Display the art in your hallway or create a Collaborative Art Show for family night.

- Save the art to revisit at the end of the year. Do the activity in June and notice how much children's skills have developed!

57

Help the Teacher

Young children love to feel they can help. It helps them feel mature and successful. So "play dumb" once in a while and invite children to help you solve a problem!

HOW-TO

1 Be dramatic! Arrive at circle time with the bag filled with art materials and a very befuddled look on your face. Say, *I have a problem. I arrived at school today with this bag full of art materials for us to do a special art project, but now I can't remember what we were going to use them for. Can you help me?*

2 Spill out the contents of the bag into the center of the circle and allow children to examine the materials. Ask: *What do you think we can make with all these things?*

3 Have children suggest ideas. Children may like to illustrate their ideas by demonstrating with the materials themselves. As children suggest ideas, write them down on chart paper and add their names. Hang the list in the art area for inspiration. Children can create their art during center time.

> **MATERIALS:** chart paper, marker, large bag filled with various items: large Styrofoam pieces, fabric scraps, aluminum foil, tongue depressors, buttons
>
> **SKILLS:** collaboration, creative thinking, expressive language, cooperation

- Remember, there is no right or wrong answer to your question. At art time, children can choose to work on their own idea, or that of someone else!

- Use this technique to introduce any art activity. Just put the materials you plan to have in the art center in a bag, and have children help you come up with an idea for a project. If you want them to make something specific, give them clues so that they can guess what it is.

Reflective Listening

An important part of feeling welcome in a group is knowing that you are being listened to. Help children learn the skill of reflective listening at the beginning of the year.

HOW-TO

1 Talk about the importance of listening and being listened to at circle time: *How does it feel when someone doesn't listen to you? How does it feel to have someone listen to you?*

2 Demonstrate how to use reflective listening. Invite a child to tell you about what they did last night or what they want to do this weekend. As the child speaks, quietly look at him. Afterward, tell the group what you heard him say: *Jimmy was telling us about the kitten that he got last night. It is black and white. Does anyone remember something else that Jimmy said?*

3 Now, invite another child to share, and say, *Let's see how well we listen. Listen carefully to Amanda, and when she is finished, raise your hand if you can tell me something she said.* Check back with the speaker to see if the children's recollections are correct. This validates both the speaker and the listeners!

MATERIALS: chart paper, markers

SKILLS: listening, expressive language, taking turns, cooperation

○ You can use a song to help this activity along:

Are you Listening?
(tune: "Are You Sleeping?")

Are you listening,
*   are you listening?*
To what (child's name)
*   has to say?*
What did s/he share?
*   What did s/he share?*
Tell us please, tell us please.

○ Use reflective listening as a "way of life" in your circle time. It will take children time and attention to develop the skill, but it will quickly become a natural part of your classroom community.

○ Apply reflective listening skills to show-and-tell activities.

Word of the Week

Part of being a community is sharing a language—learning new words together. Start at the beginning of the year by introducing a word a week.

HOW-TO

1 Choose a day of the week to be your "new word day." Tuesday is a good choice because the excitement of being back at school after the weekend has dissipated and children are more ready to focus.

2 On chart paper, write the new word. It is helpful to start with interesting adjectives because children can quickly learn how to use them in speech. Your first word might be **extraordinary**.

3 Use the word very deliberately when speaking at circle time. You might say, *I had the most* extraordinary *drive to school today.* Or, *The book we have to read today is* extraordinary *because it has illustrations that use the most* extraordinary *colors. Can you see what is so* extraordinary *about it?*

4 After you have used the word several times, invite children to suggest what they think the word means. Perhaps they can use it in a sentence, too!

5 Invite children to brainstorm a list of "Extraordinary Things" that can be added to throughout the week. Keep this hanging in the circle-time area for children to refer to. Read the list at the end of the week!

MATERIALS: chart paper, markers

SKILLS: expressive vocabulary and language, creative thinking, cooperation

Tips

- Use the word during the day to build awareness of how it is used in different contexts.

- Send a note home to families to let them know the word of the week so they can use it at home.

- Hang the word on a large sheet of paper in your writing center. Encourage children to cut pictures from magazines that represent the word.

Counting Off

The process of counting off in the circle can be difficult for young children to learn. Practice it with these fun games!

HOW-TO

1. Start by having children count off by fives while sitting in the circle.

2. Make the counting physical to help children remember the pattern. Have them take turns marching around the circle counting 1-2-3-4 (and tapping people's heads as they do so), and on 5, turn and go in the opposite direction. (This may be tricky, so model it first.)

3. When you get back to the circle, discuss which was easier, counting off while sitting or while marching? Ask, *Why?*

MATERIALS: none

SKILLS: counting, taking turns, cooperation, gross motor coordination

- For a change of pace, count off in a line. *What happens when we get to the end?*

- Change the "turn-around" number for a different experience!

1-2-3-4 Jump

Take the "counting off" game one step further in this fun counting and moving activity!

HOW-TO

1 Have the children count off by fours, going around the circle. Instead of saying the number 5, the child whose turn it is after 4 says "jump!" As the child says it, he or she jumps up and remains standing up.

2 Continue until everyone is standing up in the circle.

3 Now, reverse it! With everyone standing, count around the circle, and when the fifth child says "jump!" he or she sits down. This continues until everyone is sitting in the circle again.

MATERIALS: none

SKILLS: counting, taking turns, cooperation, gross motor coordination

Tips

● Choose five children to help you demonstrate.

● Try counting in a different language!

Follow-the-Directions Relay

Here is a fun way to practice following directions—
and to get some exercise at the same time!

HOW-TO

1 Clear some space in your circle-time area for movement. Place two chairs side by side in the circle and choose a pair of matching objects. Put one object on each chair.

2 Divide the class into two teams. One child from each team goes first. Give a three-step direction such as, "Hop to the chair, put on the glasses, and sit on the floor," then say, "Go!"

3 Send the next two out with new directions. Gradually add longer and more complicated instructions. There are no "winners," just happy participants!

MATERIALS: lively movement music, familiar objects (two of each) such as dress-up clothes, hats, fake glasses, mittens, and scarves

SKILLS: listening, following directions, gross and fine motor coordination

● Following directions is about learning sequences, and so is reading! By visually representing a song sequence for children to use, you can help children practice right-to-left progression and sequence skills. Create picture-word charts for songs such as "If You're Happy and You Know It" or "Put Your Finger in the Air," that contain "following directions" lyrics. Have children read the directions as they sing and do them!

Notes